THE
New-Now

BRIAN ROSCOE

THE NEW-NOW
COPYRIGHT © 2021 BY BRIAN ROSCOE

All rights reserved. No part of this publication may be reproduced, distributed, or transmitted in any form or by any means, including photocopying, recording, or other electronic or mechanical methods, without the prior written permission of the author, except in the case of brief quotations embodied in critical reviews and certain other noncommercial uses permitted by copyright law.

The content of this book is for general informational purposes only. It is not meant to be used, nor should it be used, to diagnose or treat any medical condition or to replace the services of your physician or other healthcare provider. The advice and strategies contained in the book may not be suitable for all readers.

Neither the author, publisher, nor any of their employees or representatives guarantees the accuracy of information in this book or its usefulness to a particular reader, nor are they responsible for any damage or negative consequence that may result from any treatment, action taken, or inaction by any person reading or following the information in this book.

For permission requests or to contact the author, visit:
brianroscoeauthor.com

ISBN-13: 978-1-957348-04-9

PRINTED IN THE UNITED STATES OF AMERICA

THE
New-Now

*The universe tirelessly conspires
to organize our lives on behalf of our growth*

Have you ever considered how often on this human journey, we're presented with new ways to see and live our lives? How many situations ,and problems are handed to us where we either immediately understand their deeper meaning and purpose, or, conversely, we completely miss the point being presented and get wrapped up in the complexity and drama of it? How often do we flat out reject any opportunity of growth, automatically, often subconsciously preferring our old thinking and entrenched positions. We can often find ourselves completely ignoring the lessons being handed to us, when we could choose to hold them, to explore them without judgment, and look with a fresh new eye, to open ourselves with a genuine curiosity to what they're offering.

We either go one way or the other depending on our state of being in the moment. But there's a clarity that unfolds for us, a support system that comes alive within us when we open ourselves to the yet unknown wisdom trying to move through us. Because no matter how big or small, all situations offer us the lessons of patience, understanding, and healing. So why wouldn't we at least try to take advantage of the opportunity?

There's a convergence that takes place between the antics of this universe and our evolving journey. This world presents our lessons, often lessons that we may not like at the time, especially some of our best, most productive and growth inspiring, albeit most difficult lessons. But we're not put here to like everything, we're here to learn, we're here to grow ourselves beyond our lessons and remember how to move into all that we can become. This is where our interest and attention should be directed, it needs to be pointed towards how we can grow in this life, how we can expand ourselves through what we've been presented. Because that's what we're meant to do, that's how we're meant to explore our journey in this life – to see even the most difficult moments of our lives as potentials for growth. That's our evolution manifesting in us through living our life. Again, it's what we're here to do.

Our true nature is realized in the foundation of knowing that we are fully alive to our human experience, awake to the intimate connection/

interaction/fusion that has always existed between our body, our mind, and our heart. And it's in this intimate relationship between the different levels of ourselves that we can touch some sense of our completion, if even only to savor it for a brief moment. And with that simple touch, we create enough of a spark within ourselves to remember the whisper of identity held in our truth. It's an identity that's one with our creation, not dependent on anything of love or fear, but saved in the knowledge of how our ideas of love and fear flow through us. In this place of life expression, there are no attachments, no aversions, just an understanding that the choices we make, whether made in love or fear, form the ground from which the quality of our life would grow. And here, we get to choose our deeper earthly experience, we get to release ourselves from anything but the awareness that this life can bring forth a knowledge of what it is to be fully alive, fully awake, and fully human. No matter what the past, the future, or even the present presents us, our identity is not held in our ideas of love or fear, but in the loving balance we hold between the two. And this is perhaps a higher form of love than mind alone can ever comprehend. This perhaps is the great love of self, an evolving love, one harmonious with the true higher journey of being human.

Forgiveness is love. **It's the end point and the beginning point for everything we do, for all that we are. And it's through the love of forgiveness that we know the most intimate identity of our own divine expression. Period!**

WELCOME TO THE NEW-NOW

you're always welcome to explore yourself

The New-Now is designed to guide you, the reader, toward your heart. Its goal is to help you remember a core part of yourself, and to help us have an authentic experience with, and knowledge of, our essence; an essence that we've somehow forgotten is a vital part of our truth in this world. And in that remembering, the hope is to inspire you to design and build a framework within that helps you hold and nurture your true identity. To understand the truth of your personal power and know your capacity to allow love to come forward at any moment and in any of its infinite forms.

The power of awakening to each moment requires us to dive deep into our core, to explore what our truth looks like, and to open up to our own unique quality of heart-centered love. This is where our self-knowledge lives, it's where our essence resides and finds its definition. Love is self-knowledge, and it represents an integral part of our journey in this world – we are always welcome to explore ourselves here.

So, explore some of the questions that awakening to yourself brings: What is it to open to the freshness your heart offers you? To walk into life without all the accumulated baggage you've collected from your time in this world? What does it mean for us to function in life from our heart, to reclaim our authentic identity, rekindle our truth, and to function in each precious and unique new moment and in the New-Now? We hold these answers within, all of us do. So, listen. The flow of life is moving through us constantly, it exists within every breath, and in every moment. So listen for the whispers within, and as you slowly remember who you are, do the work to integrate that truth into each moment of your awakened life.

Find that place within, where fear is no longer a viable option. Walk into life with the blind faith that your heart possesses all the answers to life that your mind so often misses. Remember that it's your life filtered through love, compassion, gratitude, caring, forgiveness, and any of the many qualities of love that are one with the knowledge of your heart. And know that every moment of being alive to that knowledge, awake to experiencing all that love brings, is your choice. This is where your transformation lives.

THE *New-Now*

*At some point in our spiritual evolution
we will find ourselves understanding
that our pain and our pleasure are simply
too small a theater for the intelligence
we hold in our heart.*

ALLOWING WHAT ALREADY IS

We spend so much of our lives working towards what we "think" are our dreams, but often they're not really ours. We've gotten caught up in living our lives yearning for ideas that were planted in our minds by others; driven by concepts of life that belong to society, churches, and the history of our families - caught up in the values and judgments that were passed down through a huge history of generational belief systems. And in that, we've taken for granted that life has been figured out for us. We've made the assumption that everyone around us was right, and we've chosen to believe in "I should," the directives we learned, the judgments, and shoulda, coulda, woulda's that the world taught us we had to accept. We were told to embrace ideas which guided our thinking, ideas that we were never told we had a choice about.

We never learned that there was a deeper truth to be known and explored around the concepts of success, relationships, religion, and all the things of the world that we were told to conform with. We were never told that we were also supposed to question the truth of these programs. To question and explore them from the heart and core of who we are, and that it's our destiny and our responsibility to do so.

And then when the pain and the pleasure no longer hold our attention, we start asking questions, and we find the courage to begin again. We begin our journey back to ourselves, and we question life as we learned it.

It's here that we choose new ways to think for ourselves, and we begin to breathe and move with a freshness, exploring our own ideas, listening to that quiet voice within, and opening up to our own heart-centered truth. It's here that we've chosen to live again.

Finally gaining that deeper sense of who we're meant to become, and what we are meant to do. We feed our minds through the awakening to our loving and creative hearts, remembering that we're always meant to recognize the deeper mystery of life and of being that surrounds us. And it's with this epiphany that we're honestly presented to life. It's this reconnection that draws us to the heart, puts us in a place of knowing that we are love. This is what draws us into becoming our compassion, evokes a deeper understanding of one another, it brings forth an inner desire for everyone to live fully awake and alive to themselves, and to say "yes" to their life.

This is the specialty of The New-Now. It's the unique, internal exploration of being that helps us touch what it is to be more fully alive. And as we open to it, we naturally build an ever deepening intimacy with our wondrous human journey. Recognizing that any of us only have to accept our gift, we can walk through that already opened door and return to a truth so deeply familiar us.

There's an irony to the seeking mind. So often we believe that what we are seeking is outside ourselves, and yet it's not - it never has been, nor will it ever be. The heart of waking up to ourselves is found in waking up to our own being. Becoming alive to our miracle, our creation held in this illusion of time. It's a journey of inner becoming that we'll never fully comprehend, but its purpose will always be the same. To learn love. And here, in the new-now, we're in the process of waking up to the crucial fact that we are part of this miracle, as is everyone we look at. There is no difference between any of us. And although we seem to be constantly seeking outside ourselves for that truth (it's human habit to do so), our truth and our love was placed in our being long ago, and it's simply our job is to rediscover it. Everything we need to recognize already exists within us. It's a matter of us stopping long enough to allow what already is to move through us.

Q: Are we being presented to life, or is life being presented to and through us?

A: Yes! Absolutely! Wake up to that, my friend, and this is where you find yourself, alive, within the mystery of your New-Now.

THE *New-Now*

WOW!
WHAT A RIDE!

When exploring ourselves using mindfulness as our only tool, it can have a tendency of leaving us seeing our journey through the lens of the intellect. At its more basic level, mindfulness helps us establish and cultivate an intellectual mind, a stance centered in observing the events in our world, that can result in more of an intellectual connection with our environment. There's something akin to an observer's note taking going on here, a box checking around the details of what's happening now, right in front of us and within us. And with presence, presence is more oriented around our sense of being. In it, we hold ourselves in the feeling of that ineffable connection that moves through the heart and reflects the essence of our existence. Presence helps us awaken to the quiet truth of our being in the world. It helps us recognize that as we move in the world, the world is also moving through us. And the New-Now gently helps us intertwine these two ideas. It draws us into the awareness of being alive to the heart, our heart, and awake to the deep essence of our experience in every unfolding moment. The New-Now entices us into being awake and alive to the miracle we're born to, vitally present, wired up to and almost "electrified" to what's being presented to us every instant of our life. It's a profound awakening to the light that emanates through us, and the life that unfolds within, around, and through every moment of our existence.

THE *New-Now*

The New-Now helps us manifest a deep appreciation of being alive and vibrantly connected to this world. It helps us cultivate a gratitude for our unique experience of breath and life, an embracing of what is beyond our understanding, and a waking up to an infinite life that can only be explained as pure miracle.

When we can hold the concept of the New-Now, it helps us understand that we are deeply integrated with life—not just some of the time, but all of the time—and our job is to stay awake to that knowledge as we move forward. **It's an attitude towards life itself, allowing us to see that there is truly nothing more beautiful than right now, wherever we happen to be.** We're asked to be alive to the unfolding of life, and seeing the New-Now as a form of remembering what we are. It's a shout out to the world saying, "Hey, I am alive and awake to every pinpoint of my human experience. I feel it, I'm lovingly aware of it, I am it, and it is me! Wow! What an adventure, what a beautiful, beautiful ride! Thank you! Thank you! Thank you!" This is you, opening yourself up to the breath, and the full experience of being alive to the New-Now.

"If the only prayer you ever say in your entire life is thank you, it will be enough."
-Meister Eckhart

UNDERSTANDING THE UNIQUE BLEND BEHIND *The New-Now*

The term "New-Now" is meant to impart a unique understanding of being alive to each moment in our life experience. It relates to a quality of presence to life, and a deep inner connection with ourselves as we experience being awake and alive to our world. In a very real way, the New-Now portrays an awakening to being alive to our personal part in this miracle, fully absorbed in the continuous flow of our experience right here and in this moment right now.

Being part of this world – our very presence in it and through it – suggests a profound and intimate connection with the entirety of the earth around us. Our very presence reflects a deep, almost mystical relationship with ourselves and with one another. And although the entirety of this experience is beyond our capacity to ever fully understand, its very existence and the fact that we've been given our unique role in it, automatically asks to approach our life with integrity and honor.

In light of our deep connection to life, we experience how each moment moves forward as a fresh creation, having its own wonderfully different flavor, scent, feeling, and brilliant color on every level. In being aware, awakened, and mindful of living into that never ending blend of life moving through us is to experience a very distinct understanding of being alive to the New-Now. With that understanding, we become aware that we are all very much miracles encountering an infinite journey of miracles. We are an integral part in the mystery of life touching other mysteries, continuously.

> The New-Now is both the same as and different from "presence" and "mindfulness." They all build their own unique picture of meaning in our mind around what they portray, and we can easily debate their technical meanings, impressions, and definitions. However, they're all meant to point us inward, they all hold the goal of attempting to point us toward being awake to our lives, and they all intertwine and utilize each other in their attempts at finding their own unique identity.

Yes, the deeper meaning of these three are similar. It's as though they all have the common goal of being crayons… and they each simply reflect their different colors while they exist with a common origin and function. As crayons, they add unique color, but they come from the same box.

Presence and mindfulness create a unique picture in our mind because of their historical use. And the point of creating the New-Now is to refer to a deepening and profound awareness of our human experience. The New-Now is meant to push the mindful envelope a bit farther, to help the one in search of themselves move toward an enhanced idea of their capacity of being awake and alive to life. It's meant to help us to see each moment in a fresh, more expansive, and new way. The New-Now is meant to help us to open to our life with the understanding that every moment is the creation of an experience, a happening, a precious event that will never again be experienced in exactly that same way, and only asks for our attention to it. It's life moving through us and touching our heart.

So, the New-Now naturally incorporates qualities of presence and mindfulness. When we explore the meaning that exists within the New-Now, presence, and mindfulness, each of them seem to require one another for their own definitions. You can't be present without participating in the New-Now moment in a mindful manner, just as mindfulness requires us to have a level of presence as well as being awake to the newness of each moment. And the New-Now naturally incorporates both presence and mindfulness to help spark us into being alive to life, to help us create an awareness of our miracle. It's not that any one of them is better than another, and it's not even whether we're "doing" one versus "doing" the other – it's simply that each one, in their own way, is meant to drive us in the same direction. They're all asking us to go to that place within that says, "This is who I am, this is my unique and infinite experience of being alive. Thank You."

Mindfulness, the New-Now, and Presence, or any of the concepts that we use to awaken ourselves to our lives, help us facilitate our natural ability to find and connect with a wisdom within ourselves; a wisdom centered in the heart that makes itself available to all circumstances and helps us uncover the insight that our lives are all intimately woven into the fabric of this creation.

By bringing our attention into the New-Now, we open ourselves to experience life as it unfolds – not caught in the confusion of the past, the future, or even the present, but in the constant presentation of a miracle we are intimately one with. In this quality of awakening that the New-Now sparks us toward, we claim our opportunity to be alive and awake to our lives in ways we may not have felt or experienced before. Suddenly, we see that being right here, right now, and alive to the moment in front of us, is really all we can ever truly possess in life. And as fleeting as it might seem, it's beyond brilliant as it touches us. This awakening to an awareness of our privilege to life naturally fills us with a gratitude, an appreciation, and all the feelings of the heart as no other experience can. And yet, in order to get there, we need to choose it.

As we said, awakening to the spark within every moment unfolding to us, and being truly alive to our life can't exist when we choose to live in the past, and the future is untouchable and unknowable, it's the future, it hasn't occurred yet. We can get wrapped up and lost in our past or future, but the brilliance of life gets dimmed for us when we try to live in either of those places. It's more about how we hold the past and future, the status we give them in our world. We can only fully be in and explore our journey right here, in the brilliance of the right now, and regardless of what's happening around us, despite our circumstances, we own this unfolding moment of being alive and need to treat it with a dignity.

> **Our best and only option becomes one of growing into the truth that we can only ever experience the crispness of each fresh moment in front of us now.**

It's an attitude of being in life, and it sets us up to live awakened to our experience. There's a brilliance in that understanding – a spark that we can access and live through, and with it we automatically make the choice to wake up, even just a little more, to what is.

> *"Everything can be taken from a man but one thing: the last of the human freedoms—to choose one's attitude in any given set of circumstances, to choose one's own way."*
> *-Victor Frankl*

NEW-NOW

Yes, being in the New-Now is being awake, alive, and present to a quality of life that inspires an extraordinary, almost mystical anticipation for each next moment. It's being life, present to all the thinking, all the actions and infinite qualities of participation and conscious awareness that we have access to as part of this miracle of being. In the New-Now, we're living in our willingness to embrace our journey of being, present to our aliveness in such a way that we see ourselves first as one with the miracle of life. We simultaneously become present to and wrapped up in the mystery of being awake. It's more than just a cognitive experiment; it's making the vital choice to hold our journey close and do whatever we're able to be alive to the entirety of the journey given us.

> **Within the New-Now is the realization that life is continuously changing, and that this infinite and never-ending process is ours to absorb into, experience, and cherish.**

The New-Now is the basis for showing up to life, for being present to our world. It's our ticket to genuinely experiencing all that life is offering us. It encompasses both the good and the bad of our experience, the sensations or the lack of sensation, it gives us a place to go with statements like, "I feel numb today," because we can allow ourselves to be aware of what it is to "feel numb today," to awaken to that feeling of "numb" or any other feelings. And we can do it lovingly, as a compassionate observation without the burden of having to judge it, or anything contributing to it. The New-Now allows us that presence with ourselves, that connection with our being alive and human.

And in this deep presence to life, we become more alive to the experiences of the mind; more awake to the phrases that roll through us all the time: "Something smells good," or, "Something smells bad." "Something tastes wonderful," and, "Oh! Another horrible thing!" We're left in the New-Now, alive to whatever unfolds in front of us in this miracle of being. And we can release from any attachment that requires something to look or be a specific way. In the New-Now, we can just be present to what is. No judgment, no unnecessary drama – just life unfolding while we honestly do our best to move though without defining ourselves by it.

"Being alive is the most significant phenomenon, not just on this planet, but in the whole cosmos."
　　　　　　　-Sadhguru

RELEASING PAST, PRESENT, FUTURE

In the New-Now, we release ourselves from the constraints of time. Try to remember that the past, the future, even the present, which easily becomes sidetracked into future and past, – none of them help us to be centered in this precious moment of right now, alive to the unfolding of our miracle. The past and the future will always want to breathe through us, to try and claim more life from us than they need. It's part of our human condition, they share the room with us. Our job and our challenge, while we're in that room, is to never loose track of the understanding that we are only fully alive right-here, and right-now.

Yes, even in trying to live for the present somehow allows the future and the past to wiggle their way into our memory and our thoughts and we're pulled away, distracted from our intimacy with life. Plucked away from our right here, right now, and the infinitely unfolding New-Now state of being. It's a funny thing, how as soon as we say; "I'm present", we habitually tumble into the past or fall into the future… We simply need to exclaim; "I'm alive!" And put an infinite exclamation point on it!

"Yesterday is gone. Tomorrow has not yet come. We have only today. Let us begin."
-Mother Theresa

"Drink your tea slowly and reverently, as if it is the axis on which the world earth revolves - slowly, evenly, without rushing toward the future."
-Thich Nhat Hanh

LOVE/FEAR

It's a difficult truth, but in order to see and know our love, we also need to be open to seeing and knowing our fear. And the reverse is also true; in order to fully see and understand our fear, to feel the effect it has on our life, we need to understand the depth of love that can indeed exist within us. When we're not judging either of them as good or bad, they can be seen as companions, compatriots that are simply meant to help one another reflect their momentary message of human experience. Our job is to decide which best suites us, to choose which of these we want as our inner guide.

Our right-here, right-now alive presence of mind is an invaluable asset to us as we move through life. This quality of mindfulness intimately relates to our capacity to maintain a high level of appreciative attention to what we're doing and what's happening around us. It's a reflection of our presence, of our inward movement, and it helps us clarify what it is to be awakened to our world.

We're not just subtly aware of being alive, we're deeply connected to the life held within us. We're vibrantly present to our presence, able to see our life as something more than simply the mind or just our feelings, but to claim the awakening of our heart alongside the mind, because together they are far, far more than the sum of their parts. And in our new found intimacy with every moment, and our awakened sensitivity to everything that unfolds through us, we have an understanding of what it is to be in the New-Now, recognizing not only that life is a gift but that we embody this precious gift of life.

> Be present to your world, right-here, right-now... because that's where life thrives, that's where our human experience is fullest.

LET FEAR MOVE THROUGH YOU, *not attach to you*

We all know that life naturally comes with its difficulties, and its struggles. Every one of us at some moment can find ourselves questioning the very purpose of why we're here, asking ourselves what all this craziness is about, and why life is sometimes sooo, sooo difficult. We're asking the questions put forward by anger, fear and frustration, questioning that's all too often done without the benefit of ever receiving any real answers. At least not immediately.

There's no sense in denying the struggle, getting negative about the fact that this life has plenty of difficulty and tension attached. Find some ease in the knowledge that it's part of the human condition. Just don't let the struggle of life drive your car. Fear is a natural reaction to fear-provoking circumstances. It's our teacher. So, feel it without getting stuck in it, learn from it without judging it, and move forward without believing that it was bad. Fear is simply our challenge to knowing love. It's meant to bring more meaning to the qualities of love that we can cultivate. When we don't let fear own us, there's a guidance that comes through it, and when we listen, an opportunity to gain a deeper sense of self-definition. Without understanding fear, we're emptier, and the deepest qualities of our love won't ever find their way forward.

Choose to live.
Always ask yourself:
"Will I allow outside experiences dictate my internal state of wellbeing?"

Affirmation:
"I will not allow an outside environment, experience, or circumstance to influence the integrity of my internal stance."

SATURATED...
a personal experience

There was an unexpected perk for me found in the writing of this book. While I was diligently working on trying to more fully explain this concept of the New-Now to the reader, I found myself engaging the idea in a deepening way. I experienced a kind of personal New-Now awakening in it, and found myself feeling more alive to the very experience I was trying so hard to find words for. I awakened more and more to the life I was infused with, literally walking with a refreshed attitude, and a deepened integrity towards life. I didn't have to make it happen, the attention I gave the subject simply gave it permission to evolve into and through me, as though spending so much time exploring the New-Now helped me own its message. I found myself allowing it to develop within me, not only consciously, in my intellect, but also subconsciously, as though in opening to it, I had no choice but to become more fused with it. For me, the New-Now became something akin to the backup singers for the main artist, but it became my backdrop, my supporting attitude for the path I was walking with in my world.

I found myself exploring this new way of being and felt the sense of being simultaneously awake and alive to the hidden mystery of life as well as connected to the obvious physical world I was walking in. I felt sensitive to it in every breath and noticed a feeling of oneness with everything – a kind of unity associated with the complexity held in every moment. Yup, I was doing exactly what I'm asking my reader to do, and I'm asking you, the reader, to open up to your own unique development and expanded attitude to life in the New-Now; to explore "what is" simply with curiosity, without the need to make anything happen, simply paying attention to how the experience and the preciousness of your world unfolds with infinity held within each sacred moment. I'm asking you to open up to recognizing your placement into the miracle, to allow your full presence to fuse with it. For you to be patient with the difficulties of being human, and treat yourself kindly, even through the hardening efforts of the mind. I'm asking you to awaken to the full beauty of your life, and to very honestly treat yourself as a friend.

> **Become all that you have explored, be what you have always known you are, and open up to the secrets placed in your heart. How else will you ever grow into all that you can be?**

PRACTICING PRESENCE IN *The New-Now*

Being in the New-Now is your living acknowledgment of life. It's your head bow to creation – connecting to what-is brings an honor to our place in this creation. It's the namaste of the heart. And it requires us to possess a resolute attitude of openness and a deepening awareness of our existence. Because in being alive to each moment, we're continuously waking up to life and to ourselves, sparked again and again into our experience, and into remembering what it is to be fully human. Here, we become acutely aware of being a spirit with a human form, created with feelings and senses that can only be experienced in the full presence of being alive and awake to our journey.

Describing the New-Now is kind of akin to that ancient idea of trying to describe an elephant to a blind person. It's the difference between the perception of what we can be aware of versus a complete understanding of the whole. And the elephant in the room is life's miracle. Our description is a daunting one. It's trying to explain how we can wrap ourselves around the vast qualities of the full truth of our life. The New-Now is a new approach at defining the elephant, one that we may have not previously considered. It's simply a way of helping us see our experience in yet another way, from a different angle. The hope is that through it we can expand our hearts into our journey even just a little bit more and a little bit deeper than before.

The New-Now is the same thing as mindfulness, and it's the same thing as presence, however, it provides a different, perhaps fuller, picture of what each is trying to point at. Perhaps the difference is in the fact that the New-Now does ask you to learn and draw from both mindfulness and presence for its definition. Whereas, in their very basic form, the same is not necessarily true for presence and mindfulness. Presence and mindfulness notwithstanding, the New-Now presents its own unique and robust understanding around how we can experience the deep truth that our human journey gifts us.

Mindfulness and presence can come across as being perhaps a little bland, even superficial when we're not coordinating them with seeing the depth of our life experience. Seeing it as a mystical experience, a mystery, a miracle. And that's where the new-now steps in. The new-now is where we embrace life not just as an observation, but as an unexpected gift, a new and fresh experience of what is, we simply see life with new sight. The New-Now is where we more fully engage our miracle.

THE *New-Now*

Here, in each new alive and unfolding moment, we find our ability to exist in a deeper connection with ourselves, knowing a deep and enduring gratitude for life, and feeling more awakened to our creation. We feel connected to everything alive within us right here, and right now. It's here that we embrace and honor our life, profoundly alive to every moment no matter what our miracle brings. Our opening to the New-Now affords us a space within to merge deeply into our compassion, understanding, self-love, forgiveness, and unconditional love for ourselves and others as we're moving through this world. In living awakened to the New-Now, we choose an unencumbered heart, we move forward without the need to judge life, and we embrace that connection we've reawakened within. It's a love of infinite form that can exist in all circumstances no matter what happens to be going on in our world.

INVITING PRESENCE, *Opening* TO YOUR NEW-NOW

When we can approach everything as a miracle, a new world continuously opens to us, gratitude becomes our internal state of being, and no matter what good or bad we see, we can't help but to honor the stunning beauty that continuously surrounds us all.

THE *New-Now*

Inviting this concept of the New-Now into the way we experience our life naturally pulls us into new ways of being, it helps us open up to a fresh understanding of our journey. It's through our presence to this New-Now that we open ourselves up to a more profound integration with life, being alive to everything being offered, and recognizing the freshness held in each moment. The New-Now inspires us into a fuller participation with how we notice the miracle of our own being. When we're alive, aware, and awake to the timelessness of each moment, we're alive, aware, and awake to our gift of life in this world. We're more consciously engaging life, feeling life, seeing life, sniffing, touching, and deeply sensing life. We get to experience – in a powerful way – our gift of being alive in this crazy, wonderful, awe-inspiring, and confusing extravagance we call life.

In opening to the New-Now, we're embracing life without the subconscious and semiconscious limitations and blockages that have previously influenced our world – limitations we accepted from others, society, religion, and even from ourselves. These are the inherited patterns and habits of a mind that we've acquired from a world around us, often fear-based ideas – ideas that ask us to not stand tall, to not be our truth, and not to breathe into our lives. We're asked not to love too much, being told fear was more familiar and dependable. We were seduced by those old and distorted patterns of negativity that we'd somehow come to believe we we're safer in, and that, in some way, seemed more acceptable to the world of "modern man." Controlled by blockages erected to hold us back, keep us foggy, and which encourage us to stay small. We were asked to avoid rattling the cage of life rather than encouraged to live in a fully open and big-hearted way – alive in this amazing world.

THE New-Now

Living life and connecting with this New-Now is a choice. It's choosing not to live in the fog of what you're told to think, not giving into the thinking of a fear-based environment.

> **Living life in the New-Now is the conscious act of waking up, being alive to our lives and to every moment of our own heart-centered experience.**

It's a way of bowing with honor to our own spirted evolution; a personal Namaste to being alive. Living life in the New-Now is living in the joy of being, regardless of our circumstances. It's learning how to let our thinking reflect our essence, letting our ideas move through us, free of the old, grumpy, judgment mongers whose only intention is to create anxiety, pain, limitation, and a life of shame-driven and fear-based control over our precious journey.

The New-Now presents the *opportunity* to begin again; to start every moment as a fresh experience. Your *heart* knows it. Now, convince your mind.

www.ingramcontent.com/pod-product-compliance
Lightning Source LLC
Chambersburg PA
CBHW021432070526
44577CB00001B/178